The Love of Your Life

When you get down to it, the Bible is the world's greatest book of love. Every page is rooted in the story of God's love for the people he created. The story continues with the journey of that love. Sometimes his people are wise enough to return the affection. Sometimes they learn how to love one another.

Love is supreme in this book and in our faith. No description of God is like the one that says he is love (1 John 4:8). He is just, but he is not justice. He is creative, but he is not creativity. He is love. All of creation is wrapped around the idea of God's love.

The Song is a series of materials about that subject as it relates to man and wife. But you know what we've found? We simply can't talk about marriage love out of context. It must correlate with the right kind of love between God and us. We can't afford to let God fall out of the conversation.

That's where this journal comes in. Think of it as a spiritual checkup designed to take your vital signs even as you explore the realities of love and marriage. As you think about that or any other subject, you must constantly be asking, What's going on between God and me?

This journal, if you take it seriously, can mark a breakthrough in the way you answer that question. As you encounter his phenomenal, indescribable love, you can't help but be changed. Is positive transformation worth a few minutes of each day for you? I know of one possible answer to that question, and I know that's why these pages are in your hands.

Kyle Idleman / Teaching Pastor
Southeast Christian Church
Louisville, Kentucky

Have you ever noticed how many songs are about love? It's a big, wide world; we have no shortage of topics for discussion. But when we start to sing, why is it that we find ourselves singing about love?

We smile when we watch an old, black-and-white Hollywood musical. The main character climbs onto a subway, thinks about the girl of his dreams—and breaks into song. The other passengers drop their newspapers and scowls, and they join right in! Yet there's something about this that makes sense somehow, isn't there? A soldier wouldn't break into a rhapsody, but it just seems right for a lover to do so.

It's because love and music seem to be made for each other. And who made both? God. So it's not surprising that the Bible's book of love and romance is expressed as one song: the Song of Solomon. I for one am glad it's not a lamentation.

The Song is a series of experiences created to help us understand what this kind of love is all about. There's a dramatic film for the crowd experience, a group study for a room of friends, a devotional for couples, and finally, this personal journal for the individual.

What makes this journal unique is that it's for you and God only. This is the core of everything else that will happen in The Song experience. At all the other levels, we focus on man and wife and marriage. Here we seek to find the source of power to run the marriage engine. Before we can truly love anyone else, we must know what it means to love God.

In your group and in your devotional guide, you'll work very directly on the marriage relationship. In this journal, you'll work on the God relationship in ways that are appropriate for that day's focus. For example, the first week is all about deepening our desire for each other in marriage. Here in the journal, we'll explore what it means to deepen our desire for God. The entire experience will be a dynamic encounter of building relationships vertically (with God) and horizontally (in marriage).

Warning: There's simply no way to embark on this journey without being changed forever. On the inside and on the outside, where you meet your world, you will never be the same.

So keep this journal with you as you go through the day. Read through the day's comments in the morning (that will take you only a minute or two). Then, as you go about the day, let your thoughts percolate. As opportunities arise, open the journal and write down your responses. As you turn out the lights to end another day, you'll know you have more than the daily grind to show for it. You'll have grown and changed, and your spouse will have, too. Then, in your weekly group or at church, you'll have the opportunity to go public with what you've learned in these seven days.

That's the plan. As God molds us personally, our marriages reflect it. Then our circles are blessed. And finally—the world. And that's something worth bursting into song about!

Let the music begin.

1

SESSION

DEEPENING
DESIRE

DESIRE

IT ALL STARTS WITH A SPARK.

The first chapter of Song of Solomon captures it well. Newfound love is an irresistible force. We've all experienced that pleasant tension of meeting someone and knowing that everything is different. Plans change. Priorities are rearranged. The future can no longer be considered without reference to the one with whom we've fallen in love.

It's the same when we begin to walk with Christ. Though the love is of a different variety, it has the same kind of power and pull. We desire a future with him just as we long for a future with a special person.

Just as in romance, there will be highs and lows in the relationship with Christ. Sometimes we'll feel we've grown apart. Other times we'll know we're closer than ever. In both cases, it tends to be about communication. This week we'll be thinking and praying about desire—the right kind of desire for the right kind of person and our desire for the only person who can make life worthwhile: Jesus Christ.

WEEK ONE, DAY ONE

Verse for Today:
Jesus replied: "'Love the Lord your God with all your heart and with all your soul and with all your mind.' This is the first and greatest commandment. And the second is like it: 'Love your neighbor as yourself.'"
– Matthew 22:37–38

Welcome! You're about to spend some serious time thinking, reflecting, and praying about love. Not just any love, but your love—for God and for others. How does that idea make you feel?

_____

_____

_____

_____

_____

_____

_____

_____

People have followed Christ for many reasons. Some of us were born into Christian families and never considered any other way. In that situation we would come to realize that our relationship with Christ was a kind of "arranged marriage" spiritually. True love means choosing to follow him, as we would choose to be with the human partner of our choice. Think back to the time when you chose Christ. Reflect for a few minutes on that time. What first attracted you to him?

_____

_____

_____

_____

_____

_____

_____

_____

In today's verses, Jesus laid out the top two priorities of life: loving God and then loving one another—in that order. He went on to say that every other law of life is contained within these two. Spend time today considering that concept in the context of your own life.

Your reflections on that:

_____

_____

_____

_____

_____

_____

_____

_____

_____

_____

JUST A THOUGHT

We become truly personal by loving God and by loving other humans. . . .
In its deepest sense, love is the life, the energy, of the Creator in us.
– Kallistos Ware

Ask God how you can love him more deeply today. Listen to his heart as
he tells you, and write your response here:

_____

_____

_____

_____

_____

_____

_____

_____

Lord Jesus, you are love. Everything about your life, everything about your
teaching, and everything about following you comes back to your gracious
love. It's your mission for me. I want to live it out in a far more powerful
way. Help me do that today. Show me at least one way I can love you
more deeply.

Verse for Today:

One thing I ask from the LORD, this only do I seek: that I may dwell in the house of the LORD all the days of my life, to gaze on the beauty of the LORD and to seek him in his temple.

– Psalm 27:4

Romantic love often begins with a physical attraction. It's an emotional response to the beauty of another person. It begins as a physical attraction and then becomes a deeper feeling about the love of the total individual as we come to know them better. We are also attracted to the beauty of Christ, but of course it's a different kind of beauty. The more we experience of him, the more we are attracted to his character and his love.

What do you find most beautiful about Jesus Christ?

_____
_____
_____
_____
_____
_____
_____

There is a dramatic difference between physical beauty and the beauty of the Lord. One fades with time while the other is imperishable. The only thing that changes is our ability to perceive the greatness of God as we grow closer to him. How does Psalm 27:4 demonstrate the writer's passion for the loveliness of the Lord?

_____
_____
_____
_____
_____
_____
_____

Notice the three objectives specified in this verse. What does each one mean to you? In the psalmist's world, the temple was the only place where God could truly be worshiped; today, through the power of the Holy Spirit, we can do so everywhere. What would seeking God mean in your life today and tomorrow?

_____
_____
_____
_____
_____
_____

JUST A THOUGHT

Beauty is God's handwriting.
– Charles Kingsley

Meditate on the beauty of the Lord, and tell God how you feel about that. Compose your own brief psalm about it—in your own words. It doesn't need to be fancy, just sincere.

_____
_____
_____
_____
_____
_____
_____
_____
_____

Lord, all beauty is a reflection of your beauty. I could not even tell light from dark or good from evil if I weren't made in your image. All things bright and lovely remind me of your greatness. Today, help my life to be a beautiful statement about a beautiful Lord.

Verse for Today:

How lovely is your dwelling place, LORD Almighty! My soul yearns, even faints, for the courts of the LORD; my heart and my flesh cry out for the living God.

– Psalm 84:1–2

When you fall in love with someone, you want to spend time with them. I bet you've never heard a couple say at the wedding, "We plan to have separate honeymoons." There's a self-perpetuating cycle that sets in: The more we love, the more time we want together; and the more time together, the more we love them. It's the chemistry God created for the personal fusion we call a relationship. And it's true of our relationship with him. Can you remember a time when you yearned for more time with God? What was that like?

_____

_____

_____

_____

_____

The psalmist of today's verses was clearly lovesick. He expressed deep emotion in his desire to be with his Lord. If you read the entire psalm, you'll see that he wished he could be like a sparrow making its nest near the altar! Romantic love is one thing, but what, in your opinion, would lead to someone feeling this way about an invisible God?

_____

_____

_____

_____

_____

If you're like most of us, you may be feeling a little uncomfortable about now. You might be thinking, I hurry into church late, my mind wanders during the teaching, and I forget to pray half the time. Why aren't I more like this guy in the Psalms?

Don't beat yourself up; it's called being human. But again, we observe that love, time, and presence are inextricably tied together. Making time for God leads to feeling deeper love for God. Write down one workable strategy for carving out more time for God in your life. And here's a hint: It's not all about focused Bible study and prayer at home. You can also "practice his presence" in traffic, between meetings, while showering, or anyplace else.

So what's your plan?

_____

_____

_____

_____

_____

_____

JUST A THOUGHT

What we think about when we are free to think about what we will—that is what we are or will soon become.
– A. W. Tozer

Today, refuse to focus on feelings about God. Feelings are followers—they always come behind the right kind of action. Focus instead on time spent with God. Try giving him a day in which you're aware of his presence every hour, worshiping him in your mind, asking him how he wants you to minister. Tell him below how you plan to do that:

_____

_____

_____

_____

_____

Lord, time is treasure. I realize that it's my most precious resource, and I want to lay it on the altar as a gift to you. I've come to realize that killing time is a terrible thing, because it has no resurrection. I devote this day to you. Let's live it together in joy and love.

Verse for Today:
Declare his glory among the nations,
his marvelous deeds among all peoples.
– Psalm 96:3

Love rarely makes a secret of itself. As a form of joy, it can't be contained; it tends to bubble over. If it's no more than a great restaurant you've discovered, you have to recommend it to all your friends. If it's a mate for life, all your friends and family have to know.

But what if you've met the Lord of creation, the giver of eternal life, the only one capable of transforming us into new creations? How can we keep quiet about that? To love God means to declare him before the world. It's not a matter of obligation any more than a bird feels obligated to fly or a fish to swim.

Yet we often feel reluctance to talk about our faith before others. List a few of the reasons you think this might be so.

_____

_____

_____

_____

_____

Telling others about Christ helps us to love him more. For one thing, we learn to depend upon his power for the boldness we need. Then, as we do so, we find that he gives us the words we need. Every time we declare our faith, we can feel it grow. As we pray for others to come to know him, we feel his affirmation and joy.

Today's verse is one of many that talks about declaring his glory to the nations. We want the whole world to know, but the neighborhood is a good start. The cubicle next to yours at work could be a mission field for you. Take a few moments right now to ask God to bring one person to mind, one acquaintance who needs to hear the name of Jesus this week.

List that name, along with others in your personal circle to whom you could speak.

_____

_____

_____

_____

Marriage is a public event. We invite others to the wedding so we can declare our commitment to the world. Some of us need to "go public" with our faith. That doesn't mean being obnoxious or pushy, but simply being loving and servant-hearted as we look for the right opportunity to talk about the one who lives in our hearts. How do you feel about that? What can you do to be more comfortable telling the world about your faith?

_____

_____

_____

_____

_____

JUST A THOUGHT

God directs his people not simply to worship but to sing his praises "before the nations." We are called not simply to communicate the gospel to non-believers; we must also intentionally celebrate the gospel before them.
– Tim Keller

Today, ask God to make you more aware of other people than you've ever been. Actually, the more aware of God you are, the more aware of others he will make you, because he wants to speak through you. He wants your friends to know him. Focus on service today, and give the glory to God. In the space below, tell God about your commitment to do that:

_____

_____

_____

Lord, I realize that loving you more means coming to love others more. It's only natural. Help me, then, to look at people through your eyes, to see in them what you see: lost and wandering children who can't find their way home. Give me your love for them, your moment, and your words.

WEEK ONE, DAY FIVE

Verse for Today:
For the grace of God…teaches us to say "No" to ungodliness and worldly passions, and to live self-controlled, upright and godly lives in this present age.
– Titus 2:11–12

One of the great word pictures in the Song of Solomon is that of the "little foxes" who creep into the vineyard and spoil it. The idea is that small things can become big problems in any relationship, whether it's a friendship, a marriage, or a matter of faith in God.

When it comes to being a devoted follower rather than simply a fan of Christ, the world is infested with foxes of every size. We would grow as Christians if not for this; we would serve him more fully if not for that. A time comes when we find we can no longer feel God's presence because we've let too many obstacles, too many unconfessed sins, come between us.

Why do you think it's the "little" things that cause so many big problems in faith?

_____

_____

_____

_____

_____

Paul the apostle wrote a letter to his friend Titus and spoke of the self-discipline involved in following Christ. The grace of God "teaches" us, he said. That's interesting. We aren't simply saved by Christ and left to struggle along the best we can. This is a relationship, just like marriage, and it comes with the teaching built in. And the lesson described here is one of saying "no" to ungodliness.

As you read this verse, what issues or obstacles in your own life come to mind? Spend some time in reflection, and then list at least one key issue— and describe why you think it has such a hold on your life.

_____

_____

_____

_____

"Self-controlled" means controlling our habits. "Upright" means proper or right, and "godly," of course, means God's way. Make these your three "words of the day," and think about how they would describe the situations and questions you face.

"In this present age" is Paul's way of saying right here and right now. The past is only a memory, and the future is only on the drawing board. What you have is this moment, this day. Write a few sentences telling God how you're going to enjoy a fox-free day—or as close as possible—by learning from his grace.

_____

_____

_____

_____

JUST A THOUGHT

Virtue is what happens when someone has made a thousand small choices requiring effort and concentration to do something which is good and right, but which doesn't come naturally. And then, on the thousand and first time, when it really matters, they find that they do what's required automatically. Virtue is what happens when wise and courageous choices become second nature.

– N. T. Wright

Now just spend a moment forgetting about all the hard parts and simply experiencing the goodness of God. Remember, we said this is about his grace. That means he has done the heavy lifting! It's good to plan a godly day, but don't get caught up trying it in your own strength. Celebrate God. Thank him for the classroom of today. List some of his special blessings below.

_____

_____

_____

_____

_____

_____

_____

Lord Jesus, you know how far short of perfect I fall, and you died for me anyway. You want each day to be a victory that we share in this present age. I can't imagine how or why you could love me so much, but I want to take hold of it and live this day as a celebration. I will go forward in your strength and love.

WEEK ONE, DAY SIX

Verse for Today

Clap your hands, all you nations; shout to God with cries of joy.
For the LORD Most High is awesome, the great King over all the earth.
– Psalm 47:1–2

This week we've focused on the idea of loving and desiring God. We've looked at the idea from several angles, meaning that we've come to a good time to ask the question, Are we having fun yet?

It's true. Some people focus so much on the process and the structure of following Christ that it becomes a task rather than a relationship. John Piper has said that loving Christ is a honeymoon that never ends—at least it never should. So today is a day for simply stopping to think about the greatness of God, to remember that all at once, he is the awesome Lord of the universe, great beyond our imagining—and someone who knows us and loves us better than anyone else. Have you clapped your hands about that lately?

In the space below, rewrite the two verses above in your own words. Find a new way to say what the psalmist was so excited about.

_____

_____

_____

_____

_____

Awesome has become such a casual word that it's almost surprising to find it in the Bible. We've seriously devalued it, describing a good pizza or an entertaining movie as "awesome." The dictionary defines it as "inspiring an overwhelming feeling of reverence, admiration, or fear." In other words, we are astounded. We stop breathing momentarily. We are in awe. Write the attributes of God that you find most awe-inspiring, and why.

_____

_____

_____

_____

_____

If the psalmist realized the greatness of God, he would be in awe. But it's the realization that he is our God that makes the psalmist clap his hands and shout! Our God is no uncaring cosmic force. He is love. He is Father. He is Savior and King. He calls us his own and claims the entire world as his kingdom. Not only is he infinitely beyond our comprehension, he is absolutely present and caring. Tell God how you feel about that. Don't be afraid to get excited:

_____

_____

_____

_____

_____

JUST A THOUGHT

Our God is at home with the rolling spheres,
And at home with broken hearts.
– M. P. Ferguson

It's too easy to forget that our days are battles in a war we've already won.
Christ has defeated death. He has promised us all good things. It only
remains to go out and reclaim the field for his kingdom, victory by victory.
We begin with the right mindset when we celebrate his greatness and bask
in his love. Claim this day (or tomorrow) as a victory and lay it before him
as a gift of devotion:

_____

_____

_____

_____

_____

Lord, I can think of you as the infinite, all-powerful creator, and I can think
of you as the loving Lord who walks with me. What I struggle to do is hold
both of these thoughts in my limited mind at once. Help me to worship you
for your holiness even as I accept your intimate friendship.

WEEK ONE, DAY SEVEN

As our first week comes to a close, let's use today to review and reflect,
before moving on toward thinking about increasing our intimacy with
God. Take a few moments to revisit this week's entries in your journal.
Which of the days, subjects, and Scripture passages were most helpful
to you, and why?

_____

_____

_____

_____

_____

What commitments did you make to God for your daily life this week? And how did you do in keeping them?

_____

_____

_____

_____

_____

Thinking about your daily life—apart from the journal—what was your greatest single victory this week? What would you go back and change, if it were possible to do so? Why?

_____

_____

_____

_____

_____

Thinking about the coming week, what would you like to see happen between you and God? What steps will you take on your end? What would you ask of him?

_____

_____

_____

_____

_____

In the space below, thank God for his goodness and love in the past week. Be bold enough to ask for his blessings in the week ahead. Bring him your requests, and don't forget to pray for your spouse and other people you love.

_____

_____

_____

_____

_____

JUST A THOUGHT

God's end is to enable me to see that He can walk on the chaos of my life just now.
– Oswald Chambers

God wants to do something unexpected, something magnificent, something jaw-dropping with your life. It doesn't matter how untidy or unimpressive it is. Jesus walked on stormy waters, not calm ones. He wants the same kind of miracle for your life, so that people will look and see not you at all, but Jesus on his way to teach and to love them.

Lord Jesus, thank you for the week we've had together. Like all weeks, it has been all about your perfection and my flaws. And still you love me. Still you keep leading me forward to the next week and the week after that. Thank you for the surprises that you have planned ahead. Thank you for loving me. Help me to love and desire you more than anything else in this earth.

NOTES:

SESSION

2

INCREASING INTIMACY

INTIMACY

THEY SAY THIS ABOUT HEAVEN:
Everybody wants to go there, but nobody's in too much of a hurry.

Seems to me you could say the same thing about going deeper with God. We all want that divine relationship, but too many of us are stuck in neutral. We're moving neither forward nor backward. If he is life's greatest treasure, why aren't we digging like crazy?

It's not as if knowing God is an impossible goal. You and I can grow deeper and deeper in our relationship with Christ in the same way we nurture our human relationships. It simply takes work. It takes commitment and discipline and a whole lot of patience.

Question: Do you think God is hiding from you? Any reason at all he doesn't want this thing to happen? None I can think of. He wants it and we want it. So why not make it happen?

This week, even as we think about intimacy in marriage, let's do some solid exploration of what it means to grow ever closer to God.

WEEK TWO, DAY ONE

Verse for Today:
You have searched me, LORD, and you know me. You know when I sit and when I rise; you perceive my thoughts from afar. You discern my going out and my lying down; you are familiar with all my ways. Before a word is on my tongue you, LORD, know it completely. You hem me in behind and before, and you lay your hand upon me."
– Psalm 139:1–5

I remember a song from the eighties, "Every Breath You Take" by The Police. Every time I hear it, I think, Is this guy a stalker or what? He sings about observing every little detail of the one he loves, who apparently isn't returning much of that attention.

And here we have the ancient version of that song: Psalm 139. Considering the source, I'm happy to hear it, aren't you? God cares. And by that, I mean he cares completely. He knows everything there is to know about you: your every thought, your every need. How many God-monitored aspects of your life can you count in those five verses?

_____

_____

_____

_____

_____

_____

_____

_____

The very first step in deeper intimacy with God, then, is realizing he is already there. He couldn't be any deeper and closer with you. He loves you that much. As you reflect on the implications of that idea, what does it mean for you? What do you think about God knowing your every thought and unexpressed emotion?

_____

_____

_____

_____

_____

_____

_____

You might wonder about that idea of being "hemmed in" by God. It means he's got you surrounded. You'd better come out with your hands up! "The angel of the LORD encamps around those who fear him, and he delivers them" (Psalm 34:7). So that amazing fifth verse of Psalm 139 says he is all-around you, but in a loving way. He lays his hand upon you. Have you ever felt that in a crucial moment? What was it like? Or if not, why do you think you haven't felt this?

_____

_____

_____

_____

_____

JUST A THOUGHT

We need never shout across the spaces to an absent God. He is nearer than our own soul, closer than our most secret thoughts.
– A. W. Tozer

Imagine walking through this coming day with Jesus physically by your side. He would be a part in every conversation with your friends or family. He would be there while you worked, drove, or watched television. How would this affect your life? Obviously, this is the true nature of your life with the one difference that he is not visible in a physical way. What differences can you see in your life during this day or tomorrow, if you commit to live in the reality of his presence?

_____

_____

_____

_____

_____

Lord God, you are not in hiding. You are not watching from the distance of heaven. I need to understand that you are right here and right now. You are utterly close to my every thought, utterly involved in my every daily matter. Today I commit to the knowledge of that fact and the minute-by-minute business of living out the implications. May I feel your hand upon me this day.

Verse for Today:

I will praise you, LORD, with all my heart; before the "gods" I will sing your praise.

– Psalm 138:1

As we've seen, the greatest commandment in the Bible is to love God with all our heart, mind, and strength. The tough word in there is all, especially since it's followed by a comprehensive inventory of everything that makes us ourselves. You could translate that verse as, "Give God every part of every part of you."

It comes down, then, to realizing that God has us hemmed in and surrendering. But this doesn't mean we lost; just the opposite. We're unconditionally surrendering to perfect love and peace and victory. If you consider mind, heart, and body, which part of you would be the toughest to offer? Why?

_____

_____

_____

_____

_____

_____

I think it's highly significant that the psalm speaks of praising God "before the 'gods.'" Of course, he's the only God; the others, the ones with the lowercase g, are false idols in our lives—anything we set up as a false deity. This means looking at money or power or pleasure or any of the rest and lifting up the true God right in their midst. How exactly can you do such a thing?

_____

_____

_____

_____

Why don't we know God more intimately? So much of the time it's because other things have gotten in the way. The same is true, by the way, of troubled marriages or even personal health. They suffer because of their standing on the list of priorities. To know God intimately is to love him wholeheartedly. How can you do that today?

_____

_____

_____

_____

_____

JUST A THOUGHT

[God] shows much more of Himself to some people than to others—not because he has favorites, but because it is impossible for him to show Himself to a man whose whole mind and character are in the wrong condition. Just as sunlight, though it has no favorites, cannot be reflected in a dusty mirror as clearly as a clean one.
– C. S. Lewis

You can see that the theme for this week is consistent. We want to focus on drawing closer to God, and the way to do that is to create the right conditions. So if your life is a mirror that is too dusty and dirty to reflect God, what's your first step in putting some sparkle into it?

_____

_____

_____

_____

_____

_____

Lord, I really do want to love you wholeheartedly, and I realize that before I can ever do that, I need to dethrone an idol or two. I'm thinking at this very moment of the false god that I need to deal with most. In your power and through your love, I commit to doing that today.

Verse for Today:

Before I formed you in the womb I knew you, before you were born I set you apart; I appointed you as a prophet to the nations.

– Jeremiah 1:5

Here's one to think about. Is there a gift or a skill in which you truly excel and feel a special joy whenever you're exercising it? For some, it's working with children. For others, it's music or art. Some feel truly alive when they teach or simply when they organize things. We're all different. So what is it that makes you unique? Where is the "sweet spot" of your life, the place where you come into your own?

_____

_____

_____

_____

_____

_____

_____

I want to suggest to you that God, who knew you intimately even before your birth, gave you whatever gifts or interests you have. He gave them to you so you could use them, of course. But he also gave them to you as a channel of connection to him. You have a special opportunity to connect with God when you do what he made you to do. Ask Jeremiah, who found his groove when God appointed him as a prophet. He set Jeremiah apart, we read; but he set you apart, too. Reflect on that. When do you feel closest to God? When do you feel you're doing what he made you to do?

_____

_____

_____

_____

_____

_____

Sometimes when we don't feel close to God, it could be that we've put him in a box. We expect him to show up only at church or only in a hasty prayer. When we feel delight, the channels are open. That's a great time to stop and say a silent word of thanks and praise to him. This moment is a great time, too. Tell him how you feel about the special traits he instilled in you. Also, thank him for the way he created other people you care about.

_____

_____

_____

_____

_____

_____

JUST A THOUGHT

Joy is the serious business of heaven.
– C. S. Lewis

"Every good and perfect gift is from above, coming down from the Father of the heavenly lights, who does not change like shifting shadows" (James 1:17). If you haven't experienced God in a while, let me whisper this secret in your ear: gratitude. Every good gift comes from him, so the next time you see one, acknowledge the source. When you feel joy, when you find yourself smiling, let God know you've caught him blessing you again. Why not try that right now, reviewing the good stuff from the last few days and giving him the glory?

_____

_____

_____

_____

O Father of the heavenly lights, I realize that my life is a steady outpouring of blessings. You've done so much for me that I've allowed goodness to become an entitlement for me—and that causes me to be ungrateful, which causes me to miss out on you. Let today be a steady outpouring of gratitude on my part.

Verse for Today:

Serve wholeheartedly, as if you were serving the Lord, not people, because you know that the Lord will reward each one for whatever good they do.
– Ephesians 6:7–8

We've talked about experiencing God through our personal joy. Here's another one: experiencing God through the joy of serving others. After all, Jesus made it clear that we cannot serve others without serving Christ himself. And if we love Christ, we can't help but feel led to serve others.

Think about a time when you felt really good in the midst of doing good. It could have been a big missions event, or it could have been the smallest act of kindness. When did you feel that special pleasure? How did it draw you closer to God?

_____

_____

_____

_____

Notice something about today's Scripture passage? That concept of wholeheartedly comes up again. We've thought about how God wants us to love him with all of our heart. The truth about love is that it always gets busy. Have you noticed that? Love pulls us into doing good things. How have you found that to be true? What do you think is the relationship between love and service?

_____

_____

_____

_____

We all know people who are born servants, always up to something good. But Jesus calls every one of us to develop servant hearts, because the world needs service and also because, again, it's a channel to getting to know God better. What are some key places in your life, over the next few days, when you can serve other people? Write down their names and how you'd like to serve them, and then ask God to give you courage and resolve.

_____

_____

_____

_____

_____

JUST A THOUGHT

In all of my years of service to my Lord, I have discovered a truth that has never failed and has never been compromised. That truth is that it is beyond the realm of possibilities that one has the ability to out give God. Even if I give the whole of my worth to Him, He will find a way to give back to me much more than I gave.
– Charles Spurgeon

I should mention a danger here. Some people do good things, or give money, as an investment strategy. They expect to receive credit from God or from people. There's a fine line here. We serve him obediently, but we do it for the joy of the action and for the way it brings us closer to God—not to earn points in the heavenly ledger. Ask God to purify your heart, to give you a special gift of joy in service for its own sake, and for his—with no concern for return.

_____

_____

_____

Lord, I know I can never outgive you. No matter what I do, the blessings will return to me exponentially. Yet it's a servant heart I want. I want to have the desire to give all, even if it cost me all. Today, show me every opportunity to become Jesus in the flesh for some other person, and I thank you in advance for the joy we'll share.

Verse for Today:

He says, "Be still, and know that I am God."

– Psalm 46:10

LIFE IS LOUD! More and more voices are competing for our attention in this culture. It gets to the point at which silence seems downright unnatural. We turn on the TV even if we're not watching it. Music follows us everywhere. Have you had the desire to turn down the volume lately? An unplugged vacation once a year isn't enough—you need to enter the Silent Zone on a regular basis. Stop and think: Where are the regular silent spots in your life?

_____

_____

_____

_____

_____

_____

It's easy to miss how much the Bible stresses the practice of solitude. Moses pitched a tent outside the camp as a place to meet God. Elijah found that "the Lord was not in the fire"; he entered a cave and heard God in a "gentle whisper" (1 Kings 19:12). And what about Jesus, who was so focused on preaching and healing? "Jesus often withdrew to lonely places and prayed" (Luke 5:16). Does God really need silence to be heard? Why do you think this is so important?

_____

_____

_____

_____

_____

There's something about that command from the Psalms: "Be still, and know that I am God." Two passive actions are indicated, but they are active assertions of the will. It's natural to move, but we will pause. It's natural to let the mind wander, but we will face the fact of who God is and what that means. Just hearing this verse makes me do both things. It tends to catch me just when I need it—how about you? In your experience, what kinds of things happen when you stop the perpetual motion and realize the reality of God?

_____

_____

_____

_____

_____

JUST A THOUGHT

Why is it that some Christians, although they hear many sermons, make but slow advances in the divine life? Because they neglect their closets, and do not thoughtfully meditate on God's Word. They love the wheat, but they do not grind it; they would have the corn, but they will not go forth into the fields to gather it; the fruit hangs upon the tree, but they will not pluck it; the water flows at their feet, but they will not stoop to drink it. From such folly deliver us, O Lord.
– Charles Spurgeon

Here's the big question: Once you get your hands on a little solitude, will you know what to do with it? Can you handle the idea of sitting and listening to God? It's difficult at first. Have your Bible at hand. Meditate on the Scriptures and on questions like the ones in this book. Talk to God. But learn to listen. Conversations aren't conversations unless they flow in both directions.

How are you going to put more quiet into your life—and how will you use it?

_____

_____

_____

_____

_____

You are the God of the fire and the storm, but you choose to speak to us in a gentle whisper. Lord, give me the strength to turn down the noise in my life, the "resounding gongs and the clanging cymbals"—the empty clamor of today—so that I may hear the only voice that matters. Teach me to listen stubbornly, attentively, until I have heard from you. And let that lesson begin today.

WEEK TWO, DAY SIX

Verse for Today:
But those who wait on the LORD
Shall renew their strength;
They shall mount up with wings like eagles,
They shall run and not be weary,
They shall walk and not faint.
– Isaiah 40:31, New King James Version

Yesterday we talked about stillness before God. That in itself is a challenge for the modern, activity-addicted person. But now comes the real test. "Be still before the LORD and wait patiently for him" (Psalm 37:7). I'll admit it: I struggle with stillness, but I often fail at patience. How about you?

Yet I know that great Christians throughout the ages shared one thing in common: They knew how to wait upon the Lord. That means not being moment-oriented but process-oriented; realizing that God is always at work, and that my timetable is irrelevant compared to his. Can I do that? Can you? How are you at waiting upon God?

_____

_____

_____

_____

The best motivation I can give you is to point you toward Isaiah 40:31. Have you read and reflected upon that one lately? Write down the verbs in that verse—wait, renew, mount, run, and so on—and reflect on what this means. We rail against waiting because it's passive. Yet look at the active verbs it leads to! Running; soaring on eagle wings. Write down what you feel this verse means for you at this particular point in your life:

_____

_____

_____

_____

My friend, it's so easy to struggle in the limits of our own finite ability until we run out of gas. Isaiah gives us the formula for flying high. We wait on God, building intimacy with him. That's when a power not our own begins to come upon us. What do you think it means to wait upon the Lord? Reflect for a few minutes, and then write down your thoughts. Be sure you make it personal.

_____

_____

_____

_____

JUST A THOUGHT

"Wait on the Lord" is a constant refrain in the Psalms, and it is a necessary word, for God often keeps us waiting. He is not in such a hurry as we are, and it is not his way to give more light on the future than we need for action in the present, or to guide us more than one step at a time. When in doubt, do nothing, but continue to wait on God. When action is needed, light will come. – J. I. Packer

Close today by thinking about the stuff in your life that is up in the air. What are the big issues you're facing? What are your fears? Your hopes? Have you committed these to Christ, in faith, and adopted the mindset of waiting upon him? Think of two of these issues, write them down below, and then pray about them. You can use Philippians 4:6–7 as your guide.

_____

_____

_____

_____

Lord, I need to turn from the weight of my burdens to the wait of godliness. I realize this is a wonderful path toward knowing you better, and that's really the part that matters most. I know that in the light of eternity, the issues of my life will fade like the flower. But knowing you is a forever thing. Give me the wisdom to wait.

WEEK TWO, DAY SEVEN

This has been a week for thinking about intimacy in marriage and with God. It's time to leave that topic as our focus but not as our lifestyle. Let's use today to look back and take stock.

Look back over this week's entries in your journal. Which of the days, subjects, and Scripture passages were most helpful to you, and why?

_____

_____

_____

_____

Did you make any new life commitments to God? How do you feel about these commitments? Have you shared them with anyone who might help hold you accountable?

_____

_____

_____

_____

As you think about your ordinary life activities this week, did you experience any victories? Any breakthroughs? If you could change one outcome from this week, what would it be?

_____

_____

_____

_____

_____

_____

As we face another week, do you have any specific goals for your relationship with God? What will success look like in those goals? What specific requests do you have for God about this coming week?

_____

_____

_____

_____

Take a few moments to thank God for his goodness and his love in the past week. Praise him for his faithfulness. Boldly claim his blessings in the week ahead. Spend some time committing this new week to his glory. Pray also for your spouse, family, and friends.

_____

_____

_____

_____

JUST A THOUGHT

The reason why many are still troubled, still seeking, still making little forward progress is because they haven't yet come to the end of themselves. We're still trying to give orders, and interfering with God's work within us. – A. W. Tozer

A. W. Tozer made a good point, but a tough one. The surest way to become closer to God is to come to the place where you've run out of options. It is when life totally lets us down that we discover God never does.

Yet you don't need to let that happen. God's invitation is open for you today, right now. He wants to commune with you. And you don't need to travel to a distant temple or climb some steep mountain to enter his presence. He is already here. He lives within you, and he's waiting for you to realize that and begin to live accordingly.

There's no reason in the world you can't grow closer to him every single day. Will you do that?

Lord, I've faced some powerful realizations this week. I've thought about what it means to know you intimately, and I've come to the conclusion that there is infinite space in my life to do that more fully. I want to know you and I won't settle for less.

"I want to know Christ—yes, to know the power of his resurrection and participation in his sufferings, becoming like him in his death, and so, somehow, attaining to the resurrection from the dead"
(Philippians 3:10 –11).

NOTES:

_____
_____
_____
_____
_____
_____
_____
_____
_____
_____
_____
_____
_____
_____
_____
_____
_____
_____
_____
_____
_____

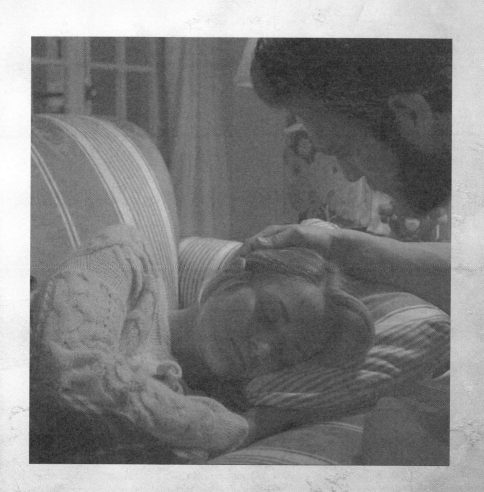

SESSION **3** **FIGHTING FAIR**

FIGHTING

**JUST AS EVERY MARRIAGE IS EVENTUALLY TESTED BY
A STORM,** so is our faith in God. It's easy to praise and worship when
the sun is shining. But what happens when life takes a sharp turn? How do
we handle it when we ask God for a bailout, and the heavens are silent?

I've been there, and I'm sure you have, too. Somehow the easy answers
aren't satisfying. When life is rough, it seems to us that faith in God should
count for something—that we ought to have a hot tip on where to find an
escape hatch.

The Bible never makes that promise. As a matter of fact, from beginning
to end it shows us godly people enduring trials. As a matter of fact, it
suggests that trials are actually good things. Again, I know what you're
thinking: Tell some guy it's a good thing when he loses his job. Tell her
it's a good thing when her husband walks out.

Truth can be difficult, but it's still truth. This week we'll explore the meaning
of tests and trials.

WEEK THREE, DAY ONE

Verse for Today:
Consider it pure joy, my brothers and sisters, whenever you face trials of
many kinds, because you know that the testing of your faith produces perseverance. Let perseverance finish its work so that you may be mature and
complete, not lacking anything.
– James 1:2–4

What's the issue for you right now? What thought puts the crease in your brow? We've all got one. Quite often we've got a nice assortment. So let's refuse to take this concept as abstract theory—let's make it personal. What is your most immediate problem—your key trial—this week? Name it and describe what it is about this issue that worries you the most.

_____

_____

_____

_____

_____

When we see a wrinkle, what's our impulse? To iron it out. We like smooth. So if you're like most of us, your natural thought is, If I didn't have to put up with this one thing, life would be awesome. And the trial becomes our enemy. That's pure human nature. What counterintuitive idea does today's Scripture passage suggest about that?

_____

_____

_____

_____

_____

Test. That's key. A trial means a problem; a test means a process toward perfection. Tests in school may be problems, but we know why we have them: so that we can grow. Have you thought of your current trial as a test? What about you do you believe is being tested? Explain.

_____

_____

_____

_____

JUST A THOUGHT

We are always in the forge, or on the anvil; by trials God is shaping us for higher things.
– Henry Ward Beecher

That idea of process is so important to our way of seeing life. It means that stumbling blocks are really stepping stones in disguise. God is ironing out the kinks. I bet you knew all this already, but I bet you'll also agree that we all need a frequent reminder.

So if this thing is a test, what will you do to pass? How are you going to get the highest grade? Write down a few ideas below:

_____

_____

_____

_____

Lord, I know that in reality I'm clay for you to mold, and everything you mold is perfect art. I need regular tests or I'll never make any progress. Help me to see every obstacle this week as another brilliant part of your plan to make me all that you want me to be.

WEEK THREE, DAY TWO

Verse for Today:
Not only so, but we also glory in our sufferings, because we know that suffering produces perseverance; perseverance, character; and character, hope.
– Romans 5:3–4

Yesterday we talked about process. What's great is that though God's purposes usually remain hidden, the process does not. The passage above from Romans is one that breaks it all down for us, from suffering to hope. Are you surprised that the end goal is hope, rather than, say, success or happiness? Why is hope an ultimate goal, in your opinion?

_____

_____

_____

_____

_____

_____

Think over your past. When was a time that you have seen this process in your life? How do you feel now about the growth you achieved? Can you see the process right now, given the issues you're facing?

_____

_____

_____

_____

_____

As you look upon your current challenges as an opportunity for God to do something exciting, what would you ask him to help you with most?

_____

_____

_____

_____

_____

JUST A THOUGHT

That man is perfect in faith who can come to God in the utter dearth of his feelings and desires, without a glow or an aspiration, with the weight of low thoughts, failures, neglects, and wandering forgetfulness, and say to Him, "Thou art my refuge."
– George MacDonald

Have you thought of God as your refuge? The greatest sign that we're building true character is when we run to him in trust and faith, rather than questioning what seems like his silence. Today—and all days—you have the opportunity to build your faith the only significant way it can be built: by obedience in the face of challenge. Write a mission statement for these next few days, acknowledging how you will prove your faith:

_____

_____

_____

_____

You are my only refuge, Lord. There is no other rock to stand upon when the storm comes. Though I may not always see your hand, I know that I can see the process. Help me to see and to glory in the work you're doing. Let me shine as a bright light during a dark time, so that others will trust you, too.

WEEK THREE, DAY THREE

Verse for Today:
Trust in the LORD with all your heart and lean not on your own understanding; in all your ways submit to him, and he will make your paths straight.
– Proverbs 3:5–6

One reason we make our problems worse is that we scramble. I know I've done that. I saw something happening that wasn't good, and I began my frantic attempts to solve the problem. Sometimes, of course, I solved it. Many other times, though, I just made things worse. The big problems defy easy answers; that's why they're big problems. Duh!

Have you been tempted to complicate your current problem, maybe take an overly easy way out or cut a corner? Have you done it in the past?

_____

_____

_____

_____

Today's passage is about the right way to handle it. Trust God. Duh #2, except isn't that a little simplistic? How do we trust God? Aren't we supposed to be willing to take action, too? Of course. These verses are more about an attitude—a perspective. Write what you think it means to trust in God rather than your own understanding. How exactly can you expect him to make your paths straight?

_____

_____

_____

_____

Sometimes it takes concentrated prayer as well as truly wise counsel. Sometimes we simply have to believe and wait. But God does speak. He does guide. Why not ask him right now to give you wisdom on how to handle the big issue you're facing this week? Write out your thoughts below and then spend time in prayer.

_____

_____

_____

_____

_____

JUST A THOUGHT

You may readily judge whether you are a child of God or a hypocrite by seeing in what direction your soul turns in seasons of severe trial. The hypocrite flies to the world and finds a sort of comfort there. But the child of God runs to his Father and expects consolation only from the Lord's hand.
– Charles Spurgeon

We've described the process by which we move from being confused children to wise believers, "mature and complete, not lacking anything," as James put it. As Spurgeon pointed out, we need to realize we've come to that point when our very first impulse, when any storm arises, is to seek God for shelter rather than the world's resources. How close are you? What progress can you see?

_____

_____

_____

_____

_____

I thank you, Lord, and I praise you. What a comfort in knowing I can lean on you rather than my own questionable resources, or those of anyone else. The wisdom and strength of my creator has been offered to me; how can I possibly overlook that and seek cheaper arrangements? Today I will find my wisdom in you, O Lord.

Verse for Today:
But he said to me, "My grace is sufficient for you, for my power is made perfect in weakness."…For when I am weak, then I am strong.
– 2 Corinthians 12:9–10

Sometimes the truth is inconvenient. It's not quite the kind of thing we believe would attract others to our faith. One of those inconvenient truths is this: God is glorified in our trials and in our weaknesses. What? How could that be? Write down some of the ways you can see how God's glory is shown in our weaknesses:

_____
_____
_____
_____
_____
_____

Amazing how often we get everything wrong. We try to show off Jesus to the world by demonstrating how strong we are, how flawless we are. And it backfires every time. We ourselves are the worst selling points for Christianity! Yet it's our weaknesses and trials that put the spotlight on the great God we serve. It is then we are forced to put our own resources aside and trust him. He gives us the grace to prevail, and it is then that the world takes note.

Who is someone in your life who may be watching as you work through a trial? How can God be glorified?

_____
_____
_____
_____
_____
_____

How can you do a better job trusting God and giving him the glory as you cope with your current challenges?

_____

_____

_____

_____

_____

JUST A THOUGHT

God did not give Paul any explanations; instead, He gave him a promise: "My grace is sufficient for thee." We do not live on explanations; we live on promises. Our feelings change, but God's promises never change. ...God did not change the situation by removing the affliction; He changed it by adding a new ingredient: grace.
– Warren Wiersbe

Grace, which God gives in abundance, is many things. It is mercy and love. It is his transforming presence. And it is the strength—not our own but his—to go through the worst and come out the best, wiser and better. Just think: He is doing that for you right now. It's enough to make you want to stop and worship, isn't it?

God of grace, I'm beginning to see myself outgrowing the stage of begging to be bailed out, begging to stay comfortable. My prayers should be for more of you, for more of your wisdom and power and love. In your grace, I promise to stop dodging inconvenience and instead to trust you and praise you right through it.

WEEK THREE, DAY FIVE

Verse for Today:
Finally, be strong in the Lord and in his mighty power. Put on the full armor of God, so that you can take your stand against the devil's schemes.
– Ephesians 6:10–11

We've put a lot of emphasis on the realization that trials are good. They're meaningful. God uses them. But we also need to acknowledge that it's not always about sitting and praying for strength. There's also what is known as spiritual warfare. Not only does God give us grace, but actual weaponry to counterattack! You can read all about it in Ephesians 6.

What are some challenges in your life you've identified as spiritual warfare—that is, genuine supernatural attacks designed to damage your faith?

_____

_____

_____

_____

Notice that we are to be strong, but in the Lord. Why is this such a critical requirement? What are some ways we mess that up?

_____

_____

_____

_____

If you're experiencing significant, truly worrisome trials right now, read Ephesians 6 and study the armor of God. (Also, be sure to see tomorrow's entry.) What are some of the key parts of the armor? How do each of them apply to you?

_____

_____

_____

_____

JUST A THOUGHT

The Christian's armor decays two ways: either by violent battery, when the Christian is overcome by temptation to sin, or else by neglecting to furbish and scour it with the use of those means which are as oil, to keep it clean and bright.
– William Gurnall

There are times for patience and waiting on God; there are other times for taking our stand and fighting back. Wisdom and discernment help us to know the difference. Think about all the current issues and relationships of your life, from marriage outward to work and friends and responsibilities. Ask God to help you be awake and ready for action.

Lord, even in times when I'm not particularly aware of spiritual conflict, I realize it's happening all-around me. I also realize I need to keep my armor strong and ready at all times. Help me to be vigilant today, spiritually sensitive to temptation and the constant possibility of poor decisions. Make me strong in you.

WEEK THREE, DAY SIX

Verse for Today:
Two are better than one, because they have a good return for their labor: If either of them falls down, one can help the other up. But pity anyone who falls and has no one to help them up.
– Ecclesiastes 4:9–10

Whom do you seek out when life attacks? Your spouse? Parents or mentors? Or do you simply internalize and try to keep up a good front?

Friendship is one more part of God's incredible array of gifts to help us handle the challenges of life. The selection of good friends is among the most important decisions you'll ever make. Apart from marriage, who is your most trusted friend? Why, and in what ways does God make you stronger through this friend?

_____

_____

_____

_____

_____

_____

_____

There is a definite limit to how many close friends anyone can have. This is why we need to choose well. What are some attributes you would look for in a close friend?

_____

_____

_____

_____

_____

Now let's turn the tables and think about what kind of friend you are. God wants to use you, just as he wants to use others in your life. What are your strongest attributes in being a supportive friend? What could afford to be better?

_____

_____

_____

_____

_____

JUST A THOUGHT

No man is the whole of himself; his friends are the rest of him.
– Harry Emerson Fosdick

Those of us with spouses and families are often tempted to "cocoon"— that is, to make little islands of our families and distance ourselves from old friends. We need each other too much to let that happen, because there are special ways that our friends can hold us accountable more so than those who live under the same roof with us. Who holds you accountable? Is there a need for stronger friendships in your life?

_____

_____

_____

_____

_____

Today I want to thank you for my friends, Lord. I pray for them by name, and I ask your blessings on them as you use them in my life. Make me a better, more sensitive, more sacrificially loving friend. And help me make one new friend today—someone who needs a friendly word.

WEEK THREE, DAY SEVEN

We've thought and prayed about trials this week from several perspectives. Let's look back and see if we can isolate the key takeaways from these days of prayer and reflection.

Take a few moments to revisit this week's entries in your journal. Which of the days, subjects, and Scripture passages were most helpful to you, and why?

_____

_____

_____

_____

_____

What was the key trial you identified on the first day? How has this trial, and your approach to it, progressed over the last several days? How have you seen God at work?

_____

_____

_____

_____

_____

Do you have any further questions about trials and tests? Any places where you need to seek counsel or clarification?

_____

_____

_____

_____

_____

Thinking about the coming week, where will you put your greatest focus in dealing with the significant trials in your life? How would you like your friends to pray for you—and when will you ask them to do so?

_____

_____

_____

_____

_____

_____

_____

In the space below, thank God for his goodness and love over the past week. Let his grace be sufficient as you trust him. Bring him your requests, and don't forget to pray for your spouse and other people you love.

_____

_____

_____

_____

_____

_____

_____

JUST A THOUGHT

This is God's universal purpose for all Christian suffering: more contentment in God and less satisfaction in self and the world.
– John Piper

Can you even imagine a world without problems? It might actually be sort of boring! There would be no real joy because we'd have nothing to compare it too, just as if there were no darkness, light would be meaningless. Crises are never welcome, but they are the very rungs of the ladder by which we climb to new heights in wisdom and maturity. They are the braces that force us to put our faith in the right place— God. As improbable as it seems, "consider it pure joy," as James put it, that God loves you enough to let you work through the tests with his help. Take these current trials and move forward with hope.

Father, it's been a week of thinking about problems, and that's never pleasant. But I'm so thankful that every problem has a context of joy; every obstacle is just a detour toward the right road. I know you're helping me find that road. Life may not be painless, but it is leading me to you, and knowing that fact leads me to worship.

NOTES:

_____
_____
_____
_____
_____
_____
_____
_____
_____
_____
_____
_____
_____
_____
_____
_____
_____
_____
_____
_____
_____
_____
_____

SESSION **4** REDISCOVERING ROMANCE

ROMANCE

I WAS LOOKING AT A SAD LITTLE GARDEN.

It was dry and withered, and insects had done their work of devastation.
I thought, Someone put a lot of care into planting these flowers.
What happened?

Relationships are like that—any and every kind. They're living things,
and they must be tended, watered, and sometimes pruned. Neglect can
be fatal. Yet no matter what, there is going to be a dry time. It's really
a question of nurture and restoration.

What about passion for God? I know what it's like to feel spiritually dry
and disconnected, and I'm sure you do, too. Please don't tell me, "Just
pray and read your Bible." I'm doing that, but the words seem lifeless.
My prayers bounce off the ceiling. Where have you gone, Lord?

And yes, I know he's never the one who has moved. I get that. The
question is, what's my move? How can I find my way back to that
intimacy with Christ that I crave? Let's do some thinking about that
this week, and see if we can't nurse a garden back to beauty.

WEEK FOUR, DAY ONE

Verse for Today:
Restore to me the joy of your salvation
and grant me a willing spirit, to sustain me.
– Psalm 51:12

Let's take your spiritual temperature. Think about the time when you were closest to God, and call that a 10. Think of the time when you were the furthest away, and make that 0. How would you rate your current spiritual passion? I know it's a lot more complicated than that, but we have to start somewhere. Think about your eagerness for worship, your attention to Scripture, and what it feels like to pray. Grade yourself and comment on why you assigned that grade.

_____

_____

_____

_____

_____

In Psalm 51, David pleaded with God for the repair of a damaged relationship. You might want to read the entire psalm. What do you notice about his words and attitude?

_____

_____

_____

_____

_____

As I read these words, I notice David's utter humility. He didn't demand that God show up and bless him; he came as a broken man aware of his own sin. Notice in this verse how he even asked God for "a willing spirit," something you'd expect him to come up with himself. He knew that every good thing comes from God. Is this a crucial point, in your opinion? Why or why not?

_____

_____

_____

_____

_____

JUST A THOUGHT

Man is spiritually dead and does not originate in himself a movement toward God and spiritual life. It's supernatural, and it is a work of divine power. Spiritual renewal accordingly is a divine miracle in which that which was dead is now alive.
– John F. Walvoord

Obviously God wants to revive our spirits; we do need to be receptive. What are some of the issues that keep us from doing that? What are the most troubling ones in your experience?

_____

_____

_____

_____

_____

_____

_____

_____

_____

Like David, I come to you with the realization of my own limitations, Father. I am totally dependent upon your love and grace. I ask you for a willing spirit, so that you may restore me to the best of our relationship. I have a prodigal spirit, O Lord, and I know you wait for me along the road. Give me the strength and desire to hurry home.

WEEK FOUR, DAY TWO

Verse for Today:
The idols of the nations are silver and gold, made by human hands. They have mouths, but cannot speak, eyes, but cannot see. They have ears, but cannot hear, nor is there breath in their mouths. Those who make them will be like them, and so will all who trust in them.
– **Psalm 135:15–18**

I truly believe the ultimate source of every problem in the world is idolatry. False gods are at war within us, vying for our allegiance. If you feel a distance between you and the true God, there's a good chance it has something to do with other things becoming more important to you, which is just another way of saying idolatry.

Honesty may be painful here, but it's essential. What are the false gods (things such as wealth, pleasure, power, love, or entertainment) you're struggling with right now?

_____
_____
_____
_____
_____
_____

What kind of specific sacrifice would it take for you to dethrone that idol and worship the one God who is real and who loves you?

_____
_____
_____
_____
_____
_____

Read the passage above. First, what observation is made about idols? Second, what does the psalmist mean when he says we "will be like them"? Spend some time reflecting on those ominous words, and write what you think that would mean in your life.

_____
_____
_____
_____
_____

JUST A THOUGHT

If revival is being withheld from us, it is because some idol remains still enthroned; because we still insist in placing our reliance in human schemes; because we still refuse to face the unchangeable truth that "It is not by might, but by My Spirit."
– Jonathan Goforth

_____

_____

_____

_____

_____

Lord, I realize that everything comes down to this one battle: dethroning every idol and giving all of myself to you. As I go through today, I ask you to show me each and every false god that looms before me. Reveal it for what it is, and give me the courage and commitment to cast it out.

WEEK FOUR, DAY THREE

Verse for Today:
As the body without the spirit is dead, so faith without deeds is dead.
– James 2:26

We like to say, "If you don't feel close to God, guess who moved." Actually, sometimes it has more to do with not moving enough. I'm talking about the kind of motion that keeps us serving others. Have you ever noticed how we feel closest to God when we're the least self-involved, particularly when we're ministering to someone in need?

Maybe there has been a time when you felt this. Describe what that was like.

_____

_____

_____

_____

I'm not saying we earn closeness to God by doing things. We can never do that. However, we can say that the best way to know Christ is to be out doing what he would be doing. Notice that James says "faith without deeds is dead." How exactly does that work, in your opinion? What is the relationship between faith and service?

_____

_____

_____

_____

In a struggling marriage, we need to get away and spend some time together. In a struggling faith, we need to spend more time with God— including the part we tend to forget; the part about serving others. How can you do a better job of that in the next few days? Be very specific.

_____

_____

_____

_____

JUST A THOUGHT

Have you noticed how much praying for revival has been going on of late— and how little revival has resulted? I believe the problem is that we have been trying to substitute praying for obeying, and it simply will not work.
– A. W. Tozer

It's kind of counterintuitive, isn't it? We figure we need to find a cave to reconnect with God. Sure, intense prayer makes a difference. But we also need to go where the needs are. When I say that word, needs, what comes to mind for the little plot of ground where God has planted you? Who needs a work of ministry? Could this be God's way of using you to fill that need?

_____

_____

_____

_____

Lord Jesus Christ, I know you've said that those who love you will be obedient to you. I also realize the kind of things obedience means in your case. I am your representative. You've placed me here to love, to help, to heal, and to point toward you. As I've read and reflected in these pages, you've put some needs on my heart. Send me; use me.

WEEK FOUR, DAY FOUR

Verse for Today:
For this is what the high and exalted One says—he who lives forever, whose name is holy: "I live in a high and holy place, but also with the one who is contrite and lowly in spirit, to revive the spirit of the lowly and to revive the heart of the contrite."
– Isaiah 57:15

This week is about dryness. That's a tough one. But are you ready for some good news? Read the verse above, and then rewrite it below in your own words. What is the good news delivered in this verse?

_____

_____

_____

_____

_____

The eternal God, high and holy, dwells with the downcast—even when he seems silent and far away. And what is he working to do? "To revive the spirit...to revive the heart." Jesus said, "Blessed are the poor in spirit, for theirs is the kingdom of heaven" (Matthew 5:3). What similarities can you find between these two verses?

_____

_____

_____

_____

_____

_____

Contrite means showing "sincere remorse." Thus God uses these lowliest of times to teach us something new. It is actually during the dry times that we learn the most and that we are driven to seek him more deeply. How can you work with God to make that happen in your life?

_____

_____

_____

_____

_____

_____

JUST A THOUGHT

I am not a theologian or a scholar, but I am very aware of the fact that pain is necessary to all of us. In my own life, I think I can honestly say that out of the deepest pain has come the strongest conviction of the presence of God and the love of God.
– Elisabeth Elliot

Faith's desert days always mean that an oasis is waiting for us. God is working to bring us a new and wonderful stage in our journey. What do you think God is preparing you for right now? Why?

_____

_____

_____

_____

_____

_____

What an awesome God you are, high and holy and yet reaching all the way down to the low and lost. Thank you for helping me to see that you are there and you are not silent. You truly love me, and your plans for me are vaster and more thrilling than I could possibly imagine. As I reflect on these things, I feel my passion for you rekindled. Help that fire to rage within me, O Lord.

Verse for Today:

When Simon Peter saw this, he fell at Jesus' knees and said, "Go away from me, Lord; I am a sinful man!"

– Luke 5:8

Yesterday's verse measured the distance between the height of heaven and the depth of our dryness. Today's verse shows the natural reaction when we suddenly perceive that distance: humility; awareness of our sin. The first time he saw Jesus perform a miracle, Peter went to the ground and pleaded with Jesus to go away. Why would he make that request?

_____

_____

_____

_____

_____

_____

_____

When we're not connecting with God, we become insensitive to our own sin condition. We're blind to the obstacles that block our fellowship with God. Then, inevitably, the greatness of God breaks through like a ray of sun, and the effect is devastating. Have you ever felt utterly humbled and deeply aware of your own issues as God revealed himself to you? How did you respond after that?

_____

_____

_____

_____

_____

_____

_____

This is the reason we often begin our prayers with worship and then move to confession. One follows naturally from the other when we have the proper perspective. Spend time right now with God, simply offering your worship and adoration. You might use Psalms as an aid. Then let him gently guide you through those sins you need to bring before him. Write below how you feel about the results of that time.

_____

_____

_____

_____

_____

_____

_____

JUST A THOUGHT

When Holy God draws near in true revival, people come under terrible conviction of sin. The outstanding feature of spiritual awakening has been the profound consciousness of the Presence and holiness of God.
– Henry Blackaby

If you study the gospels, you'll find that the most common thing people said when they saw Jesus at work was, "Have mercy!" And in that context, Jesus quite often performed a miracle! He wants to do that same thing in your life. Today, focus on the realization of who God is—and who you are. Condition your mind to the true conditions of your reality and his. Then watch for the result in how your day goes.

Lord Jesus Christ, you have forgiven me of every sin—past, present, and future. Even so, I can't simply take that for granted. I know I will still stumble, and I must bring every sin to you every single day. I know that you are faithful and not just to forgive but to draw us closer as a result. I offer today as a day of worship in all that I do. I lay it before you in the humility of self-realization.

Verse for Today:

I seek you with all my heart; do not let me stray from your commands. I have hidden your word in my heart that I might not sin against you.

– Psalm 119:10–11

There's a secret weapon for all those who want to abide in Christ as much as possible. When you commit Scripture to memory, you're giving the Holy Spirit something to work with as you go about your daily life. He will bring the right verse to mind at just the right time. Do you know any verses or passages by heart? Even the Lord's Prayer or Psalm 23?

_____

_____

_____

_____

_____

_____

_____

Never underestimate the power of God's Word, hidden in your heart. I've read stories of prisoners of war who yearned to read the Bible. Different prisoners knew different verses, and they shared them together until everyone had everyone else's verses. Then they were fortified for the crisis they were facing. List two or three favorite passages you would love to know by heart:

_____

_____

_____

_____

_____

_____

_____

Here's a bonus tip: Music is one of the most effective memory tools. So many of our worship songs have Scripture embedded in them. Learn these, too, so that you can worship no matter where you are. Write down a couple of situations in your life where you would love to be able to remember the words of Scripture, and tell how it would help you in those situations.

_____

_____

_____

_____

_____

JUST A THOUGHT

It is not the number of books you read, nor the variety of sermons you hear, nor the amount of religious conversation in which you mix, but it is the frequency and earnestness with which you meditate on these things till the truth in them becomes your own and part of your being, that ensures your growth.
– Frederick W. Robertson

We are commanded to "be transformed by the renewing of your mind" (Romans 12:2). That verse goes on to promise that if we do that, we'll be able to find God's perfect will. God is the one who does the transformation, but we can cooperate with him by feeding the right fuel to our brains. So what's your plan? Are you willing to put this to the test? How will you do it?

_____

_____

_____

_____

_____

I confess that I often take your Word for granted, O Lord. It's so accessible that I forget how blessed I am to have it. I know I have the opportunity to place it where no one on earth can take it away from me: in my heart. Sharpen my mind as I tune it to your Word, Lord. Transform me from the inside out.

So how are things between you and Christ?

We've talked about dryness this week. We've talked about renewal and revival. I'm wondering what's been going on in your mind as we've come at these topics from various angles. Have you realized the need for restoring your passion? Have you been thankful that you're closer to God than ever? Have you found ways you could draw closer? Write down a general summary of how you've responded.

_____

_____

_____

_____

Which day had the greatest impact on you? Why?

_____

_____

_____

_____

Did your time with God make a difference in how you lived this week? Why or why not? If you could do something different out there in the world, what would it be?

_____

_____

_____

_____

Bottom lining it, what will it take for you to move closer to God, other than his supernatural work in you? What steps will you take on your end? What would you ask of him?

_____

_____

_____

_____

_____

Thank God and praise him for his goodness and his love in the past week. Ask for his blessings in the week ahead. Pray for your spouse and other people you love, and ask God to make you a blessing in their lives.

_____

_____

_____

_____

_____

_____

_____

_____

_____

_____

_____

JUST A THOUGHT

When I pray for revival I pray first for the most radical thing: the utter devotion and allegiance of your hearts to Christ. That you would love Him so deeply and long for Him so passionately that His coming would be your great hope, and death would be gain, and life would be for Christ and His kingdom.
– John Piper

Reflecting on John Piper's words, we realize he's talking about something that can't be faked, something that can't be achieved through human effort. We simply need to have open and receptive spirits as he moves to transform us. May your spirit open wide.

Thank you for another week of growth, precious Lord. You are transforming me. You are showing me new realities and filling me with new hope. Yes, I do long to know you. I passionately yearn to draw closer to you every single day. Don't let my feet stray, as they're prone to do. Convict me. Speak to me. Bless me on this journey from the depths of my weakness to the surpassing heights of knowing you.

SESSION **5** **CULTIVATING COMMITMENT**

COMMITMENT

DO YOU HAVE WHAT IT TAKES TO GO THE DISTANCE?

I can think of hobbies I've taken up that consumed me—for a little while, before I lost interest and turned to something else. There are certain things, of course, that I know I'm not going to quit at any point: my marriage, my children, and my relationship with Christ. To these and a few other things, I'm committed.

Jesus once gave a warning about tower building without plan forming. The idea is that you'd better know what you're getting yourself into. Sadly, I've occasionally seen people become very excited about Jesus, sign up for every Bible study and mission project, show up whenever the church doors were open, and then do the slow fade.

Last week we focused on those dry periods and how to rekindle our faith. Those happen to everybody. But we also need to figure out the strength of our commitment, because the Bible has a few challenging ideas on that topic.

So let's seek the Scriptures and reflect deeply on the subject of going the distance and what it requires of us. Your first commitment is seven days in this journal and a series of crucial questions to ask yourself.

WEEK FIVE, DAY ONE

Verse for Today:
Commit your way to the LORD; trust in him and he will do this:
He will make your righteous reward shine like the dawn, your vindication like the noonday sun.
– Psalm 37:5–6

When you first became a believer, someone probably explained your commitment to follow Jesus. If you've ever joined a church, your first official action was probably to fill out some kind of commitment card or form. Think back to those times. What did it mean to follow Christ, as far as you understood it in the beginning?

_____

_____

_____

_____

What has time added to your understanding? How would you now define being a fully committed follower of Jesus Christ?

_____

_____

_____

_____

We're actually talking about a two-way commitment—that is, a covenant. According to the verse above, you commit your "way" (your life and strategies and values) to God. What commitment does he make to you? Express the promise of that verse in your own words.

_____

_____

_____

_____

JUST A THOUGHT

If you do not plan to live the Christian life totally committed to knowing your God and to walking in obedience to him, then don't begin, for this is what Christianity is all about. It is a change of citizenship, a change of governments, a change of allegiance. If you have no intention of letting Christ rule your life, then forget Christianity; it is not for you.
– Kay Arthur

High stakes, when you think about it. You give your life and all that it involves to God—"all" is a small word with a big meaning. At the same time, his reward to you—the life you end up with—"shines like the dawn." To me, that's the most beautiful and hopeful time of the day. It's newness. It's the majesty of a sunrise. It's the most energetic time. This is how the world sees you: bright and brilliant and full of life. Ask God to make you shine like the dawn today:

_____

_____

_____

_____

_____

_____

_____

Lord, I do want to shine like a fresh morning in a twilight world. I want your truth to be vindicated, as the psalm says, like the sun at noon on a summer day. I realize I'm committing everything, but my life is such a small gift compared to the commitment you make. I promise to live this day on your covenant. Shine through me.

WEEK FIVE, DAY TWO

Verse fot Today:
"Choose for yourselves this day whom you will serve, whether the gods your ancestors served beyond the Euphrates, or the gods of the Amorites, in whose land you are living. But as for me and my household, we will serve the LORD."
– Joshua 24:15

Joshua stood before his people as they looked upon their future. He made an incredible point: They would make a choice one way or the other. As Bob Dylan sang, "you're gonna have to serve somebody." It's not as if we have the ability to live no-commitment lives. That kind of independence doesn't exist. You will be committed to something. One thing to rule them

all, so to speak. Reflect on this verse and concept, and write down several
of the important commitments in your life.

_____

_____

_____

_____

_____

_____

The idea of godly commitment is that your ultimate allegiance is to the
Lord. What effect would that have on your other various priorities? Would
it mean, for instance, that everything else is completely unimportant?
Why or why not?

_____

_____

_____

_____

_____

_____

Earlier in this journal we thought about idolatry—placing anything in your
life in God's place. We are married, but he or she is not our god. We have
a career, but it's not our god. Let's revisit this issue in your life. What is the
single greatest challenge to God's place in your life?

_____

_____

_____

_____

_____

_____

JUST A THOUGHT

Your commitments can develop you or destroy you, but either way,
they will define you.
– Rick Warren

Someone said, "You are what you eat." I would add that we become what we follow. Each choice in that direction will shape us. What choice can you make right now, as a promise before Christ, to be a true, fully committed follower of him?

_____

_____

_____

_____

_____

_____

_____

The psalmist said, "Search me and know my heart," dear Lord, but I realize all too well you've already done that. You know what really matters to me. And what I know is that I can't be a fully committed follower of Christ and something or someone else. Guide me in the lifelong process of overthrowing the pretenders to the throne of my life. Starting today.

WEEK FIVE, DAY THREE

Verse for Today:
Therefore, since we are surrounded by such a great cloud of witnesses, let us throw off everything that hinders and the sin that so easily entangles.
– Hebrews 12:1

Who are the people who truly inspire your life? List the most important ones, and describe what about them inspires you.

_____

_____

_____

_____

_____

_____

_____

Hebrews 11 is a short essay about heroes of faith, and the point is that they lived without the model of Christ before them—a model we'll talk about tomorrow. Hebrews 12:1 gathers those heroes into a "great cloud of witnesses" who cheer us on like fans at a big game. Of course, we need to read and reflect on Scripture to get their encouragement. How has the Bible energized you in your commitment to Christ?

_____
_____
_____
_____
_____
_____

There is also a cloud of negative witnesses—everywhere. How can we attune ourselves to the encouragers of life while being strong in the presence of all the negative messages about Christ and about life?

_____
_____
_____
_____
_____
_____
_____

JUST A THOUGHT

This is the way all the witnesses of Hebrews 11 are helping us. They have gathered along the sidelines of our race and they hold out their wounds and their joys and give us the best high-fives we ever got: "Go for it! You can do it. By faith you can finish. You can lay the weights down and the sins. By faith, by the assurance of better things hoped for, you can do it. I did it. And I know it can be done. Run. RUN!"

– Ray Stedman

You are running a relay race with, so far, a two thousand year course. The last generation handed you the baton, and you must one day hand it to those who come behind you. How does this knowledge encourage your commitment? What can you personally do to internalize the idea that you aren't running a lonely race?

_____

_____

_____

_____

_____

Thank you for those who encourage us "in the cloud," Lord! You have given us an extensive record of faith heroes, and you have placed among us living examples of what it means to run the race with passion. May your Spirit whisper in my ear, keeping me from slowing down, fixing my eyes on the finish line, helping me throw off the sin that entangles. Help me to run with excellence today.

WEEK FIVE, DAY FOUR

Verse for Today:
Fixing our eyes on Jesus, the pioneer and perfecter of faith. For the joy set before him he endured the cross, scorning its shame, and sat down at the right hand of the throne of God.
– Hebrews 12:2

Christianity is no casual option. We are asked to commit everything we are and will be. But an example is set before us. The gospels make it clear that Jesus chose the cross. He knew what lay ahead of him, but he led his disciples to Jerusalem and submitted to the most awful death imaginable— and he did it for us. As you think about Jesus' commitment to you, how does it affect your commitment to him? Why?

_____

_____

_____

_____

The verse above directly follows yesterday's verse. Not only are we encouraged by the examples of faith heroes. There is Jesus himself, our "pioneer and perfecter of faith." In other words, God gave us the ultimate model, the pacesetter in this human race. What are some ways you can set the example of Christ before you to inspire your own courage and commitment?

_____

_____

_____

_____

_____

_____

_____

_____

According to the verse, commitment brings a reward. What is it? How does it translate for us, in your opinion? You might refer to Ephesians 2:6.

_____

_____

_____

_____

_____

_____

_____

_____

JUST A THOUGHT

You never hear Jesus say in Pilate's judgement hall one word that would let you imagine that he was sorry that he had undertaken so costly a sacrifice for us. When His hands are pierced, when He is parched with fever, His tongue dried up like a shard of pottery, when His whole body is dissolved into the dust of death, you never hear a groan or a shriek that looks like Jesus is going back on His commitment.

– Charles Spurgeon

Jesus was "all in" with his commitment to us. It extended to his verbal forgiveness from the cross of the men who murdered him. He didn't merely teach his message in the abstract; he lived it in the flesh, in the toughest of environments. As you look at your current life, how are you doing in the "live it out" department? What actions can you take to deepen your commitment to Christ?

_____

_____

_____

_____

_____

Lord Jesus, you were utterly obedient to God, even when that meant being obedient to the cross. You are not only the perfecter; you are the pioneer. That means you have blazed a trail designed for my feet. I can't know what crosses that trail may lead to, but I, too, want to be able to say, "It is finished" one day. I want to hear your voice saying, "Well done, faithful servant." I commit my life to your path.

WEEK FIVE, DAY FIVE

Verse for Today:
See to it that no one takes you captive through hollow and deceptive philosophy, which depends on human tradition and the elemental spiritual forces of this world rather than on Christ.
– Colossians 2:8

"The spirit of the age" is a seductive force. It's so difficult to notice simply because it's the conventional wisdom of the day. Jesus spoke of a narrow road that leads to life and a broad road that leads to destruction (Matthew 7:13–14). People get their rules for life from all kinds of sources. What are some examples of "hollow philosophies" that you observe?

_____

_____

_____

_____

How can empty teaching damage our faith commitment? What are some of the things we can do to avoid its influence?

_____

_____

_____

_____

_____

_____

Commitment to Christ is commitment to God's laws, which can be very challenging these days. "Truth decay" is a serious problem. What will you do to strengthen your grip on the truth revealed through Scripture?

_____

_____

_____

_____

_____

JUST A THOUGHT

The world is characterized by the subtle and relentless pressure it brings to bear upon us to conform to its values and practices. It creeps up on us little by little. What was once unthinkable becomes thinkable, then doable, and finally acceptable to society at large…Christians are no more than five to ten years behind the world.
– Jerry Bridges

We need to learn to think biblically, to evaluate what we see in the world based on biblical principles—rather than mold the Bible to fit the world— and yet live as appealing witnesses to the truth of Christ, rather than flee to a Christian-only commune. Quite a challenge! What do you see as the keys to modeling the faith in a world moving in the opposite direction?

_____

_____

_____

Lord, I commit myself to your Word, and to living it obediently. I want to enter through the right gate, even if the world calls it "narrow." I will listen to your Spirit as he lives within me and helps me to test the spirits in everyday life. I will follow you, wherever your path may lead.

WEEK FIVE, DAY SIX

Verse for Today:
But from everlasting to everlasting the LORD's love is with those who fear him, and his righteousness with their children's children—with those who keep his covenant and remember to obey his precepts.
– Psalm 103:17–18

As we think about going the distance, committing to Christ for a lifetime and for all eternity, the idea of the future should encourage rather than frighten us. For one thing, we know everything is in God's hands. He will use even the lowest moments for our good and his glory. We know we will experience more growth, more joy, more fruit. But we also know we're leaving a legacy for our children and our children's children. What are some of the various legacies—physical and otherwise—you plan to leave behind you?

_____

_____

_____

_____

_____

_____

The verses above say that God's love is forever. Maybe "you can't take it with you," but you can leave an incredible wealth of spiritual treasure. For our children, God continues to bless the work of our lives. What kinds of things can we do to leave a spiritual legacy?

_____

_____

_____

_____

The legacy we leave doesn't have to be complicated. How is it described in the latter part of verse 18, and what does that mean to you?

_____

_____

_____

_____

_____

JUST A THOUGHT

You cannot see faith, but you can see the footprints of the faithful. We must leave behind "faithful footprints" for others to follow.
– Dennis Anderson

What if you don't or won't have children? The principle still holds true. We are creating a future, one human being at a time, all the time. Your life is not merely your own. The present moment is only a prelude. We need to have a vision to leave, with our lives, a signpost to the kingdom of God for future generations. How do you feel God is leading you to do that?

_____

_____

_____

_____

_____

Give me "faithful footprints," Lord. Everything about our culture teaches us to live selfishly. You teach us to lay down our lives for one another, including those who aren't even alive yet. Make my life a legacy that pleases you. Give my name the quality that when people speak it one day, they think of you.

WEEK FIVE, DAY SEVEN

Wow! What a week, thinking about the costs and benefits of commitment. As I've worked on this journal, I've seen so many new paths for reflection in my life. I trust and pray the same has been true for you.

Review this fifth week in your journal. Which days, subjects, and Scripture passages were most helpful to you, and why? Which ones might you memorize?

_____

_____

_____

_____

Did you make any new life commitments to God? How do you feel about these commitments? Have you shared them with anyone who might help hold you accountable?

_____

_____

_____

_____

_____

How did the week go in terms of your everyday responsibilities and relationships? Any blessings to be thankful for? Any new trials or tests on the horizon? If you could change one outcome from this week, what would it be?

_____

_____

_____

_____

_____

With one week to go in this journal, do you have any specific goals for your relationship with God? What will success look like in those goals? What specific requests do you have for God about this coming week?

_____

_____

_____

_____

_____

_____

Take a few moments to praise the name of Christ for his full and sacrificial commitment to you. Exalt him for following his path that was as narrow as a cross. Commit to serve him joyfully, gladly, and courageously in the coming week. Offer this new week to his glory. Pray also for your spouse, family, and friends.

_____

_____

_____

_____

JUST A THOUGHT

A mother warned her son, who was entering the Air Corps, "Son, fly low and slow." It was foolish advice. Aviation requires speed and altitude for safety. There must be complete renunciation of the earth for the sky, or tragedy may result.

Just so, the Christian life requires a clean break with earthbound thinking, and a complete committal to that which is heavenly. Life is an unproductive affair for many Christians because they are clinging too close to shore; they have not launched "out into the deep" at the word of the Master.
–Walter L. Moore

I've seen too many earthbound Christians—would-be eagles who stroll down the sidewalk rather than streaking across vast and lovely skies. We try to take it slow. We try to go easy on the altitude. Yet God promises to renew our strength, to make us soar like eagles and run without weariness. (Isaiah 40:31). What are we afraid of? Why won't we commit?
To switch metaphors, do you remember leaping into the pool for the first time? You just couldn't do it halfway. You can't do this halfway, either. Christ is calling you to spread your wings and fly.

Lord, I've been in the shallow end of the pool for too long. I want the thrill of the depths. I have nothing to lose but my weariness, my confusion, and the burden of my sins. Today I make a fresh commitment to following you wherever you lead. Guide my steps. Lead me where you will.

SESSION

6

FOSTERING
FAITH

FAITH

SOME SAY FAITH IS A PRIVATE ISSUE.

Sure, the same way an infectious disease is a private issue. Faith is infectious, too; it's just the opposite of a disease.

Faith is a highly contagious case of hope, the hope coming from the fact that it's based on fact and connects ordinary people with supernatural power. God never says, "Here, keep it to yourself." He bestows his blessings with the instruction of spreading them as far and as wide as possible.

During these weeks, we've explored our relationship with God, and all of its roads lead to a single destination: bearing fruit. Jesus said, "I chose you and appointed you so that you might go and bear fruit—fruit that will last" (John 15:16). He did something eternally significant so that we could do things that are eternally significant. He didn't come to give us information or even good worship times; he came that we might have life.

So on this final week of our journal, we'll explore what that life is all about. What kind of fruit are we to bear? How does it grow? Let's find out.

WEEK SIX, DAY ONE

Verse for Today:
This is to my Father's glory, that you bear much fruit, showing yourselves to be my disciples.
– John 15:8

Based on your past knowledge, how would you define the word fruit as used by Jesus in the verse above?

_____

_____

_____

_____

_____

These words were spoken in the upper room, a few hours before Jesus was arrested and crucified. He knew that the end of his earthly ministry meant the beginning of the disciples' work. The verse indicates that fruit-bearing shows people to be followers of Jesus. So we should think about Jesus' own understanding of the term. Based on his actions in the gospels, how do you think he understood the word?

_____

_____

_____

_____

_____

We know that Jesus taught and healed. We also know that he showed what love was all about, and he gave himself for others. What are some ways we should be doing those things today?

_____

_____

_____

_____

_____

_____

_____

JUST A THOUGHT

God wants spiritual fruit, not religious nuts.
– Anonymous

There is always a delicate balance between faith and works—that is, between a relationship with God and work for God. Different people balance the equation in different ways. When all is said and done, we can agree that we're expected to do both—to know God well and to serve him effectively. Reflecting on your current life, where do you do the best at serving him? Where are you the least fruitful?

_____

_____

_____

_____

_____

_____

Lord Jesus, the fruit you bore was our salvation. You changed the world forever, and I know that you expect us to do the same. I can do nothing without you and everything in the power of your Spirit. Help me to understand, on a daily basis, exactly how I can bear fruit here and now and ultimately forever. Help my every endeavor to remind the world of you, and to give you the glory.

WEEK SIX, DAY TWO

Verse for Today:
Remain in me, as I also remain in you. No branch can bear fruit by itself; it must remain in the vine. Neither can you bear fruit unless you remain in me. I am the vine; you are the branches.
– John 15:4–5

As Jesus spoke more intimately than ever to his disciples over that final meal, he gave them an amazing word picture to understand what it meant to be his follower: vine and branches. Based on John 15:4, what was the "aha" moment, the key concept, that he was teaching?

_____

_____

_____

_____

We make the mistake of thinking of ourselves as self-sufficient vines in our own right, and we forget the life-giving substances flow through us from Christ alone. Have you ever operated in that way? What was the result?

_____

_____

_____

_____

_____

"Remain (or abide) in me," Jesus said. This is also a highly significant statement. We don't check in with Jesus, we stay connected permanently like branches on a vine. How exactly do we do that?

_____

_____

_____

_____

_____

JUST A THOUGHT

It is not the bee's touching on the flowers that gathers the honey, but her abiding for a time upon them, and drawing out the sweet. It is not he that reads most, but he that meditates most on divine truth, that will prove the choicest, wisest, strongest Christian.
– Joseph Hall

Why do we accomplish so little for Christ? Does it mean we need to work a little harder? No. Does it mean we need to pray or study the Scriptures a little longer? Not necessarily. It means we need to abide with Christ more deeply. We need to reconnect with him and receive his power, which we cannot manufacture no matter how clever or determined we are. How deeply have you learned to abide? How can you enhance your connection?

_____

_____

_____

_____

Lord Jesus, it's so clear that this is one of the most important ideas ever entrusted to us. I need to talk less and listen more. I don't need to leave you behind when I go forth into the world; I need to seek your power and presence to accompany me. I need to let my spirit linger in your love and your mercy and your grace. Today I will abide with you and allow you to grow the fruit.

WEEK SIX, DAY THREE

Verse for Today:
He cuts off every branch in me that bears no fruit, while every branch that does bear fruit he prunes so that it will be even more fruitful.
– John 15:2

Sometimes "branches" are cut away. It happens when they were bearing no fruit, which indicates they were never really connected to the life-giving vine. More important for our consideration, there is a pruning process. Based upon your understanding of gardening, what is Jesus referring to as "pruning" in John 15:2?

_____

_____

_____

_____

_____

Our lives are crowded, overcommitted, and often poorly prioritized. Jesus told us he will help us cut away the portions that bear no fruit. As believers mature, we see them focusing more intently on the work that is their true calling and dropping the empty activities. How do you think Jesus wishes to prune your activities?

_____

_____

_____

_____

Pruning isn't some kind of punishment; it's simply about increased fruitfulness. Imagining your life with a greater focus upon the matters that are most important, how do you envision your life? What would your fruitfulness look like?

_____

_____

_____

_____

_____

_____

JUST A THOUGHT

Were you ever in a greenhouse or in a vineyard at the season of cutting back the vines? What [scandalous] waste it would seem to an ignorant person to see scattered on the floor the bright green leaves and the incipient clusters, and to look up at the bare stem, bleeding at a hundred points from the sharp steel. Yes! But there was not a random stroke in it all, and there was nothing cut away which it was not loss to keep and gain to lose; and it was all done artistically, scientifically, for a set purpose—that the plant might bring forth more fruit.
– Alexander MacLaren

If you're currently in a season of growing more attentive to God and more obedient to his purposes, you probably already feel the sharpness of the gardener's shears upon your life and activities. Don't fight it. Cooperate with Christ as he shapes you to move from a handful of fruit to a basket, and from a basket to a fragrant orchard. Talk to God about it right now, and express your impressions of his will in the space below:

_____

_____

_____

_____

_____

Dear Jesus, I know that growing in wisdom always means growing in discernment of my own life. Pruning is painful—and beautiful. It results in the pure joy of fruitfulness, and it inspires celebrations in heaven. I want to be more fruitful. On this day, help me be the wisest possible steward of my time and purpose.

WEEK SIX, DAY FOUR

Verse for Today:
If you remain in me and my words remain in you, ask whatever you wish, and it will be done for you.
– John 15:7

Have you ever wondered about those mysterious biblical promises that every prayer will be answered? We've seen otherwise! Painfully so. Today's verse sheds a little light on an important question. What is the one thing that makes the difference in our prayers? Why is this so?

_____

_____

_____

_____

_____

_____

_____

Two conditions, both involving "abiding," are given. What is the result of his words abiding in us? How can we make that happen?

_____

_____

_____

_____

_____

_____

_____

_____

As you seek to pray more in the will of the Father, how can you structure your prayer time to make better use of this principle? In other words, what should you do in the first portion of your prayer? How should it develop from there?

_____

_____

_____

_____

_____

_____

_____

JUST A THOUGHT

Prayer is the natural out-gushing of a soul in communion with Jesus. Just as the leaf and the fruit will come out of the vine without any conscious effort on the part of the branch, but simply because of its living union with the stem, so prayer buds and blossoms and produces fruit out of souls abiding in Jesus. As stars shine, so do abiders pray.
– Charles Spurgeon

Are you hesitant to pray? Not sure how to be effective at it? Prone to a wandering mind? When you abide with Christ, the problem will be solved. The closer you feel to him, the more you'll find yourself praying so that it's no more of a task or discipline than eating a meal—just something you'll do as you feel the hunger for it. A good beginning is letting his words find a home in our hearts, so that they come quickly to our minds. Write out what you would like to see happen in your prayer life:

_____

_____

_____

_____

_____

_____

_____

How lovely is this idea of abiding, Lord Jesus. My spirit remains in you and your words remain in me—a marriage of spirits. You invite us to come unto you and rest, because we work too much at these things. Prayer becomes hard labor. Faith becomes guilt. Then we wonder why we bear no fruit. Abide in me, dear Lord. Help me to abide in you. May I spend all of this day in the knowledge that we are together.

WEEK SIX, DAY FIVE

Verse for Today:
The gospel is bearing fruit and growing throughout the whole world—just as it has been doing among you since the day you heard it and truly understood God's grace.
– Colossians 1:6

If we abide in Christ, we find our horizons growing all the time. We care about the entire world because he cares about it. We long for everyone to know him, no matter where they live, and we begin to focus on the Father we have in common rather than the petty things we don't. In the past, how have you thought about missions? How has your faith shaped your attitude toward people in other walks of life, whether locally or internationally?

_____

_____

_____

_____

_____

_____

Paul the apostle wrote the words above from Colossians. According to him, what aspect of God must we understand before we begin to see the gospel spreading throughout the world? Why would this be so?

_____

_____

_____

_____

_____

No one can honestly read and reflect on the gospels without concluding that Jesus wants us to bear human fruit. And how can they hear if no one tells them? What options are open to you for being involved in bearing fruit through sharing the gospel?

_____

_____

_____

_____

_____

_____

_____

JUST A THOUGHT

Some wish to live within the sound of church and chapel bell. I want to run a rescue shop within a yard of hell.
– C. T. Studd

Why do you think so few Christians are effective in sharing their faith? How will abiding in Christ make a difference—in your life in particular?

_____

_____

_____

_____

_____

_____

_____

_____

How I long to stand before you one day, Lord Jesus, with those I have invited into your kingdom. I realize I cannot and will not accomplish this unless I am filled with your presence. I need your courage. I need your words. I need the opportunities that you will bring, if only I have a willingness to cooperate. Show me this very day someone who needs a word about you.

Verse for Today:

But the fruit of the Spirit is love, joy, peace, forbearance, kindness, good-ness, faithfulness, gentleness and self-control.

– Galatians 5:22–23

There is one more kind of fruit described in Scripture: the fruit of Christian character. Paul lists nine signs that we have been abiding in Christ. Again, these are fruit—they grow naturally rather than through effort of any kind. Have you seen these begin to come forth and ripen in your life? Describe your observations.

_____

_____

_____

_____

_____

_____

Every personality is different. Some are naturally gentle, for example, while gentleness is a tough one for others. Some struggle with self-control or love. Which of these fruit seems the most elusive to you? Have you talked with God about it?

_____

_____

_____

_____

_____

How would your life, your goals, and your relationships change if these fruit began to develop more rapidly? Give specific examples of things that could happen.

_____

_____

_____

_____

JUST A THOUGHT

Have you ever noticed that along the banks of a stream the vegetation is always abundant and luxurious? This is what the Bible says about us. As the Holy Spirit flows freely in our lives, a rich and beautiful character grows. We are filled with love, with joy, with peace. In every relationship we exhibit that patience, kindness, goodness, faithfulness, gentleness, and self-control that mark us as God's own.
– Larry Richards

How can we possibly measure an inner relationship with God? Perhaps we can't, but we can certainly look for these nine "leading indicators" that his presence within us is making a greater difference. It would be "fruitless" to strain and strive for any of these nine, but growing closer to God is the answer. Talk to God about these things. Write down what you decide in terms of things you need to change.

_____

_____

_____

_____

_____

_____

_____

_____

Here, Lord Jesus, is a picture of you painted in only nine words. These are traits to be admired throughout the world, and yet they are uncommon in any corner of it. Only in you can we attain the growth of these treasured marks of character. I yearn to grow into them, dear Lord. May this day show, through my actions, that I know you better than I did yesterday.

WEEK SIX, DAY SEVEN

We've come to the end of this journal about growth in our relationship with God. Let's look back and see if we can isolate the most powerful ideas that we can incorporate into our lives, starting with this sixth week. Take a few moments to revisit its entries in your journal. Which of the days, subjects, and Scripture passages did you find the most striking, and why?

_____

_____

_____

_____

_____

Having made this study of fruitfulness, what comes to your mind in your own life when you hear the term? What kind of fruit do you believe God wants you to bear?

_____

_____

_____

_____

_____

Spend a bit of time reviewing all the weeks together by checking the "Day Seven" page of each, where you drew conclusions. Which week stood out the most for you? Write below your intention for making changes in your life, based on that week's thoughts.

_____

_____

_____

_____

_____

Think of two or three other changes you feel you need to make, or reflections you need to keep close to your heart, based on your work during these weeks. Also, write down the name of an accountability partner—someone with whom you'll share your commitment, and who will make sure it doesn't fade from your life.

_____

_____

_____

_____

Address God below in a declaration of dependence upon him, making a covenant based on what you've written in the items above. Spell out what you'd like to see happen in your life, and ask him to provide the answers, the power, and the courage. Below it, sign your name.

_____

_____

_____

_____

_____

_____

_____

_____

_____

_____

JUST A THOUGHT

I have come home at last! This is my real country! I belong here. This is the land I have been looking for all my life, though I never knew it till now. ...Come further up, come further in!
– C. S. Lewis

If you've come to this page without shortcuts, and if you've worked through other parts of The Song series at the same time, you've read many Bible verses, asked yourself many questions, and reflected on many life-shaping issues. The question now is this: What will be the fruit of these weeks? Will you simply hoard new information in your mind and feel smarter, or will you leverage what you've learned and live more wisely? My prayer is that you've come to a deeper knowledge of God, a stronger commitment to your marriage, and a more profound vision of your place in this world. These pages may come to an end, but our God never does. You will never open any door through which he cannot or will not follow you. May his presence empower you, and may his love remake you as we all march one day at a time down the road that leads to our final and joyful destination.

NOTES:

NOTES:

NOTES:

NOTES:

NOTES:

INSPIRED BY THE SONG OF SOLOMON

THE SONG

EVEN THE WISEST OF MEN WAS A FOOL FOR LOVE

THESONGMOVIE.COM

IN THEATERS SEPTEMBER 26

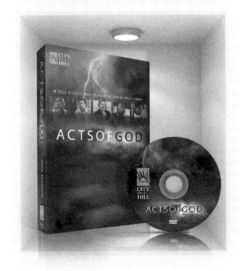